THAT'S LIFE, SNOOPY

by CHARLES M. SCHULZ

Selected cartoons from
Thompson Is In Trouble, Charlie Brown, Vol. 2

A FAWCETT CREST BOOK

Fawcett Publications, Inc., Greenwich, Connecticut

THAT'S LIFE, SNOOPY

This book prepared especially for Fawcett Publications, Inc., comprises the second half of THOMPSON IS IN TROUBLE, CHARLIE BROWN, and is reprinted by arrangement with Holt, Rinehart and Winston, Inc.

Copyright © 1972, 1973 by United Feature Syndicate, Inc.

ISBN 0-449-22886-X

Printed in the United States of America

10 9 8 7 6 5 4 3 2 1

Dear Miss Sweetstory,
I suppose you have heard about the banning of your book from our library.
Well, I just wanted you to know that I am fighting for you. I have even hired an attorney.
"THE SUPPRESSING OF EVIDENCE OUGHT ALWAYS TO BE TAKEN FOR THE STRONGEST EVIDENCE!"
Such as he is.
SCHULZ

Reason for writing Book _I wrote from a sense of need. I needed something to do. You can't just sleep all day long._

I was one of eight Beagles. We had a happy life. Lots to eat and a good cage, although looking out at the world through chicken wire can get to you after awhile.

Married _Almost once, but that's a long story._

Schools and Colleges attended _Obedience School dropout._

Suggestions for Promotion _If you don't promote my book, I'll get another publisher so fast it will make your head spin._

I LIKE FILLING OUT QUESTIONNAIRES!

Pay to the Order of Me!
money, money, money $ and more money
Linus Van Pelt
HA!! LOOK AT THAT!
IT'S STARTING TO SNOW, AND I'M READY!
I'M GOING TO BE THE FIRST KID IN THE NEIGHBORHOOD TO SHOVEL WALKS..
I'M GOING FROM HOUSE TO HOUSE, AND I'M GOING TO SHOVEL EVERY SIDEWALK AND DRIVEWAY THAT I CAN FIND!

English Theme
"The True Meaning of Christmas."
To me, Christmas is the joy of getting.
YOU MEAN 'GIVING'... CHRISTMAS IS THE JOY OF GIVING....
I DON'T HAVE THE SLIGHTEST IDEA WHAT YOU'RE TALKING ABOUT!
SCHULZ

Ten milligrams equals one centigram.
Ten decigrams equals one gram.
Ten grams equals one grampa.
KEEP GOING... I CAN HARDLY WAIT TO SEE WHAT COMES NEXT...
SCHULZ

THE PEANUTS GALLERY

includes: